Alice's Attic
295-1602

To: Ann Kelly
Xmas-'94

D0252920

Wedgwood Jasper

Robin Reilly

Wedgwood Jasper

The World Publishing Company
New York

Published by The World Publishing Company

Published simultaneously in Canada
by Nelson, Foster & Scott Ltd.

First American Edition 1972

Copyright © the collective work Charles Letts and Company Limited 1972
       © text Robin Reilly 1972
       © illustrations Charles Letts and Company Limited 1972
All rights reserved
Library of Congress catalog card number: 75–170320
Printed in Great Britain

WORLD PUBLISHING
TIMES MIRROR

Contents

Wedgwood Jasper

INTRODUCTION

In England the second half of the eighteenth century was a period of invention, development, and expansion, unsurpassed by any in her history. The traditional enterprise of the middle-classes formed a partnership with aristocratic patronage; creative genius attracted private encouragement and investment; initiative and endeavour were seen to be rewarded. In this period an empire was established, and Britain's supremacy at sea exposed opportunities for increased trade which could not be exploited without organized industries. Even the loss of the American colonies raised hopes of a new market for British goods, potentially greater than any in the world. It was, above all, an age of opportunity, favouring the rise of men equipped to take advantage of it.

Josiah Wedgwood has been called 'the father of English pottery', but it would be more accurate to describe him as the founder of the British pottery industry. Before his birth the making of pottery in England was little more than a peasant craft; at the time of his death it had been transformed, largely through his extraordinary endeavours and achievements, into a great industry, and the international reputation of his firm could stand comparison with those of Meissen and Sèvres.

Born in Burslem in 1730, Josiah was the youngest of the twelve children of Thomas and Mary Wedgwood of the Churchyard Pottery. The family had been craftsmen potters for at least three generations and the Churchyard Works had been built by Josiah's great-grandfather; but profits were small in the Staffordshire potteries, ranging from about £90 to £300 a year, and few 'pot banks' employed more than ten men. With some exceptions these produced an uninspired assortment of black, brown and red mugs, jugs, and butter pots, made from local clays, and a small quantity of salt-glazed stoneware. Domestic earthenware for the table was almost unknown: food was served on wooden platters, or plates of pewter, silver, or imported porcelain, according to the wealth of the household. In domestic terms the introduction of moderately priced white or cream-coloured earthenware for the table was as revolutionary as the invention and development of plastic.

At the age of six Josiah Wedgwood began his education, walking seven miles each day to attend school at Newcastle-under-Lyme; but three years later, on the death of his father, he went to work for his eldest brother, Thomas, who had inherited the family pottery.

At fourteen he was officially apprenticed to his brother to learn 'the Art, Mistery, Occupation or Imployment of Throwing and Handleing', though he was handicapped by an infection in one knee (probably 'Bridie's abscess') resulting from an earlier attack of smallpox developing into osteomyelitis. This later caused him to have the leg amputated under the supervision of Dr. Erasmus Darwin. When, in 1752, Josiah was refused a partnership by his brother, he joined John Harrison for two unsatisfactory years at Cliffe Bank. In 1754 he was taken into partnership by Thomas Whieldon of Fenton, at that time the most creative potter in Britain.

Whieldon was then chiefly concerned with the manufacture of cheap white stoneware, and earthenware pieces decorated in uneven shades of brown known as tortoise-shell. These were somewhat experimental, the random streaked patterns being formed by the fusing into the glaze of powdered metal oxides dusted over the surface before firing. Wedgwood undoubtedly benefited greatly from Whieldon's superior knowledge and experience, and it was while he was at Fenton that he began his own experiments 'to try for some more solid improvements as well in the Body as in the Glazes, the Colours, and the Forms, of the articles of our manufacture . . . I saw the field was spacious, and the soil so good, as to promise an ample recompense for any one who should labour diligently in its cultivation'. These led him, soon after starting his own pottery at the Ivy House in 1759, to the perfection of a rich dark green glaze, which he could use to decorate earthenware in imitation of the fashionable cauliflower, pineapple, and cabbage shapes produced in soft paste porcelain at Chelsea following the early Meissen porcelain of the Baroque period.

Queensware

In 1762 Wedgwood moved to the Brick House (later known as the Bell Works because workmen were summoned by bell instead of the horn customary in the district) where he manufactured 'useful wares' for the following eleven years. It was there that he first produced what he described as 'a species of earthenware for the table, quite new in appearance, covered with a rich and brilliant glaze, bearing sudden alterations of heat and cold, manufactured with ease and expedition, and consequently cheap'. He studied the designs and shapes not only of the oriental and continental porcelain manufacturers but also of the great British silversmiths of the period, and by adapting these for use in his own *creamware*, created a new range of tableware priced for all but the poorest class but beautifully made and elegant enough for royalty. In 1767 he wrote: 'The demand for the said *cream colour* . . . still increases. It is really amazing how rapidly the use of it has spread almost over the whole globe, and how universally it is liked.' By command of Queen Charlotte it was renamed *Queensware* and, in 1774, it was used for the largest and most celebrated of all Wedgwood's commissions, a dinner and dessert service of nine hundred and fifty-two pieces for the Empress Catherine of Russia.

Black Basalt

Parallel with his experiments to create a new tableware, Wedgwood was also

8

working to improve the crude 'Egyptian Black' stonewares already made by a number of the Staffordshire potters. The new *Black Basalt* developed by him bore little resemblance to the wares which inspired it: fine-grained, smooth, and richer in hue, it was a particularly handsome medium for fine classical vases, and suitable also for bas-relief plaques, busts, medallions, cameos, and figures, in addition to 'useful wares' for the table. It was undoubtedly the success of his black basalt which revealed to Wedgwood the extent of the market for purely ornamental ceramic wares. It brought him, also, many of the influential patrons who were to play so prominent a part in the later production of jasper. Of black basalt Wedgwood wrote in 1773, 'The Black is sterling and will last for ever', a bold prophecy which has been amply justified by the continuing popularity of this beautiful ware during the past two hundred years.

Thomas Bentley

The life and work of Josiah Wedgwood owed much to the influence of two people: his wife, Sarah; and his partner, Thomas Bentley. Wedgwood had met Bentley, a prosperous Liverpool merchant, on one of his visits to the transfer printers, subsequently Sadler & Green, in 1762. The two men formed an intimate and lasting friendship and, in 1769, after several years of negotiation, they signed the deeds of a partnership which was brought to an end only by Bentley's death eleven years later. Bentley's taste, knowledge of the arts, and social contacts, were of inestimable value to Wedgwood, most particularly in the design and marketing of ornamental wares which became Bentley's special respon-

sibility. In 1769, also, Josiah formally opened his new factory named *Etruria*, built on the Ridge House Estate between Hanley and Newcastle-under-Lyme. He had acquired this estate for three thousand pounds three years earlier. Six 'First Day's' black basalt vases were thrown by Wedgwood himself, with his new partner, Bentley, turning the potter's wheel, to commemorate the event.

Sarah Wedgwood

Sarah Wedgwood was Josiah's first cousin, whom he had married in 1764. A shrewd, devoted, and considerate woman, her practical judgment was of much assistance to him in the design of 'useful wares' for the table. Josiah acknowledged this in a letter to his partner: 'I speak from experience in Female taste, without which I should have made but a poor figure among my pots, not one of which of any consequence is finished without the approbation of my Sally.'

Jasper

Josiah Wedgwood's Queensware was, without question, his greatest achievement and contribution to the pottery industry; his improved black basalt was in the forefront of the revival of classicism in ceramic form and ornament; but his outstanding creation, the triumphant outcome of more than ten thousand recorded experiments, was his invention of *Jasper*. The long and arduous search for perfection in an entirely new and original ceramic body sprang, oddly, from Wedgwood's desire to compete in the rapidly expanding market for imitations and reproductions of Graeco-Roman bas-reliefs and intaglios. He embarked upon it with his customary enthusiasm as an interest which might prove profitable; it became for him an absorbing and driving passion, perilously near to mania. In January, 1771, he wrote to Bentley, 'I am making new Experiments with several different objects in view . . . first to make a white body, susceptible of being coloured & which shall polish itself in burning Bisket'; but three and a half years later he was complaining, 'If I had more *time*, more *hands*, & more *heads* I could do something—but as it is I must be content to do as well as I can. A Man who is in the midst of a course of experiments *should not be at home* to anything, or anybody else but that cannot be my case. Farewell—I am almost crazy.'

The vast range of jasper ware produced during the past two hundred years, and the smooth-running jasper production line of the Wedgwood factory today, using streamlined, but in all essentials the same, manufacturing methods as those of the first Josiah Wedgwood, obscure the complexity and labour of his task.

In the circumstances of eighteenth-century manufacturing, to improve upon an established product was complex enough; but Wedgwood was experimenting with materials never recorded in use, materials of which little or nothing was known and for which there were but primitive methods of chemical analysis. It is not surprising, therefore, that much of Wedgwood's frustration arose from a simple confusion between two forms of barium: sulphate of barium, known locally as 'cawk' and later used in the preparation of the pigment called 'permanent white'; and carbonate of barium, which was to be found locally in small quantities in

its native form of witherite. His records of experiments are sufficient witness to his labours, but it is in his letters to his friend and partner, Thomas Bentley, that he reveals his human reactions to continuing stress: the burning hope extinguished by countless failures, and the indomitable determination to succeed which rekindled the flame.

On the 7th March, 1774, more than three years after his first mention of a new 'white body', he writes: 'I have for some time been reviewing my experiments & I find such *Roots*, such *Seeds* as would open & branch out wonderfully if I could nail myself down to the cultivation of them for a year or two. And the Foxhunter does not enjoy more pleasure from the Chace . . .', but four months later he is experiencing more trouble with his materials: 'They have plagued me sadly of late. At one time the body is white & fine as it should be, the next we make perhaps, having used a different lump of the Spaith [barium] is a cinamon colour. One time it is melted to a Glass, another time as dry as a Tob[acco] Pipe. . . .' In August he is 'almost crazy', but by the 3rd September is able to write, 'I believe I shall make an excellent white body, & with *absolute certainty* without the fusible spath.'

No precise date can be given for the invention of jasper. The name is first mentioned by Josiah in a letter to Bentley dated 27th November, 1775, but it is clear that jasper was in limited production at least three months earlier. Some confusion arises also from a widespread failure in the past to understand that Wedgwood's exhaustive experiments resulted in the invention and production of two separate but very similar ceramic bodies. He describes them himself in the sixth and final edition of his *Catalogue*, printed in 1787:

(*i*) 'White porcelain biscuit, with a smooth wax-like surface, of the same properties as the basaltes except in what depends on colour.'

(*ii*) 'Jasper—a white porcelain biscuit of exquisite beauty and delicacy, possessing the general properties of the basaltes, together with that of receiving colours through its whole surface, in a manner which no other body, ancient or modern, has been known to do. This renders it peculiarly fit for cameos, portraits, and all subjects in bas-relief; as the ground may be made of any colour throughout, without paint or enamel, and the raised figures of a pure white.'

The earlier 'waxen' body is smooth, hard, white, and like earthenware densely opaque. Cast or turned, it lacks the crispness of detail always evident on the finest jasper, which is often, like porcelain, translucent. Jasper, incomparably the finer product, and also the most consistent and versatile, rapidly superseded the earlier invention which was gradually withdrawn from production. Later, a white 'dry body' earthenware was produced. This was porous and thus must always be glazed if the article was intended to hold liquid. Although often decorated with coloured reliefs, its soft, porous composition and the frequent use of a 'smear' glaze producing a total effect much like the use of salt glaze on a white stoneware, readily identifies it and differentiates it from either jasper or the earlier 'waxen' white body. The dense, porcellaneous, non-porous jasper body required no glaze, which would merely have blurred the crisp definition of the bas-relief decoration or engine-turned patterns. A highly-polished finish is, nevertheless, often found on the edges of cameos and medallions, and—though more rarely—on their upper surfaces. It is also to be found occasionally on the inside of cups and bowls, and the rims of cups, bowls, and saucers. This finish is the product of lapidary polishing, and it is one of the unique qualities of jasper as a ceramic body that it is capable of being polished in the same manner as the gem stones it was intended to imitate.

On the 1st January, 1775, Wedgwood wrote confidently of both the 'white body' and also of a 'blue body', which he mentions for the first time. He adds, 'I have likewise a beautifull Sea Green, & several other colors *for grounds* to Cameos, Intaglios &c.' In fact his troubles were not over: the jasper body continued to be fugitive and capricious but he was already impatient to reproduce in the new, coloured jasper many of the cameos, portrait medallions, and plaques already available in basalt, and to add to the range of models and designs.

From 1776 until his death in 1795, much of his boundless energy was poured into establishing the new product in a bewildering variety of objects. Cameos were used in settings (many of them superbly finished in cut steel by Boulton and Fothergill) for such diverse objects as buckles, bracelets, brooches, and bell-pulls; swords, daggers, and door-handles; coat-buttons, rings, opera glasses, and smelling-bottles; coach panels, window-shutters, chatelaines, snuff-boxes, grand pianos, chests of drawers, and hat-pins. Larger jasper pieces include candlesticks, plant pots, portrait medallions, plaques or 'tablets', tea-ware (though probably no set larger than the *cabaret à deux*, comprising a teapot, sugar box, and cream jug, two cups and saucers, and an oval tray), figures, busts, and models of animals (very rare), and, after 1780, vases.

Artists and Modellers

Although many of the forms and designs used by Wedgwood were 'taken from the antique', the introduction of jasper created a greatly increased need for artists and modellers. Of those employed at Etruria the most successful were William Hackwood and Henry Webber; but there were many others employed temporarily at the factory, or in London or Rome, or commissioned for special projects, among them John Flaxman, George Stubbs, John Charles Lochée, Joachim Smith, Lady Diana Beauclerk, Lady Templetown, Miss Crewe, and John Devaere. Other artists who supplied Wedgwood with designs, moulds, casts, or bas-reliefs in wax or sulphur included Matthew and Isaac Gosset, James Tassie, and John Bacon. Even the great Sir Joshua Reynolds, first president of the Royal Academy and the most famous painter in England, allowed Wedgwood to use designs after his paintings and helped in recommending artists and with criticism of his work.

William Hackwood

John Flaxman, later recognized as one of the most gifted British sculptors of the time and a member of the Royal Academy, was responsible for some of Wedgwood's most distinguished plaques, cameos, and portraits; but it was the work of Hackwood, and of the consistently reliable and highly-trained Webber, head of the modelling studio at Etruria from 1782 until 1794, which formed the cornerstone of the bas-relief production. From a humble start, hired as an assistant modeller in 1769 and doubtfully permitted in 1771 to attempt the portrait of the young Master Crew, Hackwood rapidly made himself indispensable. The vigour and the fine detail of his modelling (particularly evident in undercutting) are in no way inferior to the best of Flaxman's work, and the portrait of Edward Bourne (Plate 5) is unsurpassed in the quality of modelling by any in the long list of Wedgwood portrait medallions. William Hackwood continued to work at Etruria until 1832, completing an astonishing sixty-three years of service to the firm. In July, 1776, Wedgwood was already wishing 'we had half a dozen more Hackwoods'. Rather less impressive were the modelling services of the rogue Voyez, sacked by Wedgwood before he had completed his first temporary contract; and of the pathetic itinerant Mr. Tebo, whose attempts at modelling heads of hares were described witheringly by Wedgwood as 'like the head of a drown'd Puppy' and 'full as like Pigs as Hares'.

The Portland Vase

Tragically, Thomas Bentley, whose good sense and good taste contributed so much to the early success of jasper, did not live to see it reach its peak of perfection in the form of vases, for he died in 1780 before any were completed. Nor did he see the Wedgwood Portland Vase, which Josiah considered his greatest achievement. The vase shown in Plate 1 (Frontispiece) is Wedgwood's copy sold to Thomas Hope of Amsterdam in 1793, possibly No. 2 from the first edition.

Of the original Portland (or Barberini) Vase, probably the most famous vase and the finest example of Greek cameo-glass in the world, almost nothing is known for certain before it was catalogued in the collection of the Barberini family in 1642. Modern research suggests that it was made in Alexandria about 50 B.C. and that it was originally of *amphora* shape. Acquired from the Barberini family in about 1780 by James Byres, it was sold to Sir William Hamilton who disposed of it, presumably with his customary profit, to the eccentric Duchess of Portland (described by Walpole as 'a simple woman, but perfectly sober, and intoxicated only by *empty* vases'). Two years later, following her death, it was bought in, at the auction of her collection, by the third Duke. Within three days it had been borrowed by Josiah Wedgwood who had obtained permission from the new owner to make replicas of it in jasper.

For the next four years Wedgwood, his son Josiah II, Henry Webber, and William Hackwood were constantly employed in experiments with the jasper body to arrive at the particular deep blue-black of the original glass, in preparing working drawings of the vase, which must be returned to the Duke within twelve months, and in making models of the cameo relief subjects. After many trials and failures, the first successful copy was finished in October 1789. The first edition of copies for subscribers and for presentation to patrons, friends, and museums was begun in 1790. The fifteenth copy, admired by Queen Charlotte, was submitted for expert opinion to Sir Joshua Reynolds.

On the 15th June, 1790, he gave it his certificate: 'I can venture to declare it a correct and faithful imitation both in regard to general effect, and the most minute details of the parts.'

The original Portland Vase, on loan to the British Museum, was smashed by an Irishman in 1845, apparently for the insufficient reason that he was drunk. Twice repaired, the vase was finally restored to some semblance of its original appearance by using Wedgwood's copy, presented to the British Museum, as a model.

The Portland Vase and its copies are surrounded by unsolved mysteries: the early history of the vase, prior to 1642, is not known: the subject and meaning of the relief groups have defied the most scholarly researches, though there has been no lack of imaginative theory or unsupported speculation; the shape of the vase, considered by many to be aesthetically unsatisfactory, is probably not the original, and the enigmatic base cameo must therefore be a later addition; and there is not even any certainty about the number of copies made by Wedgwood in his first edition, the production of which included a small number in slate blue and continued for nearly forty years.

There were several later editions, for the most part remarkable only for their clumsiness and lack of all but a superficial resemblance to the original. For the 1839 edition, in deference to a public taste zealously guarded against the spectacle of frontal nudity of whatever classical respectability, the figures were draped, an addition which does nothing to disguise the coarseness of the modelling. Other Wedgwood editions since 1880 included various sizes in all colours, the latest being a small quantity in solid green and white jasper in 1957.

Whether or not one regards the Portland Vase as an artistic masterpiece, the quality of the cameo-cutting is of the finest; nor can there be any doubt that while the triumph of Wedgwood's invention was the creation of jasper, it was in the production of his copies of the Portland Vase that he reached the peak of that triumph.

The Portrait Medallions

If the first copies of the Portland Vase were the most significant of Wedgwood's productions in jasper, the most interesting were undoubtedly the portrait medallions. The idea of relief portraiture was not original: the art of portrait modelling in wax had been known for two thousand years and practised by such great artists as Michelangelo and Cellini. The demand for likenesses which could be duplicated cheaply for distribution to the public or to members of the family revived interest in this fragile art. This was an atmosphere in which the inventor of a more permanent material for reproducible relief portraits might thrive, and Josiah Wedgwood and James Tassie separately recognized the opportunity. This potential market was greatly enhanced and increased by the fashion for collecting classical cameo and intaglio gems. Both Tassie, with his 'glass paste', and Wedgwood, with his jasper, exploited the market fully.

Cameos and intaglios in basalt or biscuit earthenware were among the earliest productions at Etruria, and the perfecting of jasper enabled Wedgwood to add greatly to their range and immeasureably to their appeal. It has, indeed, been urged that the portrait medallions are the most aesthetically satisfying of all Wedgwood ware. The 1779 Catalogue lists more than two thousand cameos and intaglios, and large sets of small medals and medallion portraits of 'Kings and Illustrious persons of Asia, Egypt and Greece', 'Heads of Illustrious Romans', the twelve Caesars and their Empresses, the fifty-two Emperors from Nerva to Constantine the Great, two hundred and fifty-six Popes, and the rulers of England and France. The vast number of these miniatures is astonishing enough, but it is the superlative quality maintained throughout the list which baffles the imagination. Grant describes them as an 'armée d'élite', an army composed of lilliputians each as perfect in itself as the 'David' of Michael Angelo or as Salisbury Cathedral'. Nowhere was this quality more apparent than in Classes X and XI of the Catalogue, the 'Heads of Illustrious Moderns from Chaucer to the Present Time' which was divided into sections of 'Poets'; 'Painters, Philosophers, Physicians etc.'; 'Divines, Artists, Antiquarians, Poets etc.'; and 'Princes and Statesmen'. Though some of the earlier 'Moderns' were largely imaginative portraits, many more were modelled from medals, portrait paintings or engravings, and a number of contemporaries were modelled from life. Several of Wedgwood's portraits are the only authentic and contemporary likenesses of their sitters now available. In size the oval medallions vary from about 2″ to 11″ in height, but the majority are about $3\frac{1}{2}″ \times 2\frac{1}{2}″$ and the largest are exceptionally rare. Wedgwood produced portraits of the famous, which he thought would have a commercial appeal and value, but he also accepted private commissions and, largely for this reason, some remain unidentified. Tassie supplied a number of the models and there are thus a few portraits which exist both in jasper and glass paste. Other original portraits were modelled by Flaxman, Hackwood, Lochée, Joachim Smith, the Gossets, and John Devaere.

The Wedgwood medallions comprise, without doubt, the largest and most uniquely interesting series of historical portraits ever undertaken in any medium. The early examples, finely undercut, are also strikingly handsome, and it is not surprising that they are now among the most sought-after and expensive of all Wedgwood ware. In them are combined simplicity, beauty, outstanding craftsmanship, human and historical interest, and rarity, and they will certainly continue to appreciate in value. Many of the original moulds still exist at the factory, and replicas of the early portraits have occasionally been issued. A small number of original portraits has been added during the past hundred and fifty years, including the British sovereigns, allied war leaders in 1918, American Presidents, and Sir Winston Churchill. These modern portraits are not, as a general rule, undercut.

Josiah Wedgwood himself died in 1795. He was succeeded by his son, Josiah II, now understood to have been one of the most consistently underrated potters in the history of the industry, in partnership with Thomas Byerley, Wedgwood's nephew.

Wedgwood after 1795

For the collector the most desirable Wedgwood jasper has always been considered to be that made during the first Josiah's lifetime (prior to 1795) and, in cameos, medallions, and plaques, most particularly those marked 'Wedgwood & Bentley' indicating that they were produced prior to 1780. This has led to the mistaken assumption that any vase of fine quality must necessarily be 'first period'. In fact it is not difficult to prove that Josiah II added substantially to the variety of shapes available in 1795, and many of the finest vases belong to the period when he was in charge of the firm. The quality of Wedgwood's jasper suffered little, if at all, in the first thirty years after the death of its creator.

For a time both the quality and popularity of jasper declined. Later in the century many new shapes were added and new colours attempted. There was little of any particular distinction or special artistic merit or originality, but there were some interesting experiments and the traditions and techniques were preserved. The excesses and vulgarity of ornament which recommended themselves to other pottery manufacturers following the Great Exhibition (1851) appear to have left no mark on jasper production at Etruria, though other departments did not escape altogether unscathed.

It is too often assumed that the date of manufacture of a piece of Wedgwood is the prime consideration for a collector. On the contrary this information is relevant only as an indication of a period of artistic and technical excellence. It is primarily the visible and tangible quality of a piece which determines its value, though of course—for such is the snobbery of the market—rarity and changing fashion will affect its price. Originality of design is not necessarily an important factor as it might be in other forms of art: jasper, as a ceramic body was original; but the majority of the designs used for its ornamentation were not. It is, however, possible to use jasper in a manner not immediately reflecting the neo-classicism of the eighteenth century (Plate 58). It is also possible to produce limited quantities of pieces of exceptional quality: limited by the time and expert craftsmanship required in their production, and therefore too highly priced for distribution in large numbers. It is time for a revaluation of the best of the jasper produced during the last century; and the work of Bert Bentley (Etruria 1891–1936), a craftsman of exceptional skill, and of Harry Barnard (employed 1896–1933), the inventive potter-historian of Wedgwood, is already becoming important to collectors although produced within the past sixty years.

There are many who emulated Wedgwood: the jasperware of the Turner and Adams factories, in particular, was often of a quality which would have satisfied even Josiah Wedgwood, though there is no evidence that the prospect of competition alarmed him. Nor should the imitations or the copies alarm the collector. Even a brief study of Wedgwood will convince him that, as Barnard has written, 'Wedgwood cannot be faked'.

Two of the most important collections of Wedgwood jasper are preserved at the Wedgwood factory at Barlaston and at the City of Nottingham Museum and Art Gallery. With a single exception, all the pieces illustrated are from these sources. The author acknowledges with gratitude the co-operation and assistance given to him by Josiah Wedgwood & Sons Ltd., and by Mr. E. J. Laws, Director of Museums, and Mr. David Phillips, Keeper of Art, at Nottingham Castle.

Some of the pieces illustrated are of such rarity that they are unlikely ever to come within the grasp of the collector; but it is only by a study of the finest examples that the student may learn about Wedgwood jasper. Almost alone in the entire field of collecting, jasper has been continuously in production, and by the use of the same methods, for nearly two hundred years, and it is not possible to put a precise date upon every piece. Marks may be helpful, but real understanding comes from the study of reference books and the practical application of this background theory to examples in museums, in the auction rooms, and in the shops of reputable dealers. There is no substitute for practical examination with the eyes and, whenever this is permitted, with the hands.

By itself, no book, however comprehensive, can provide many of the answers; it is the hope and intention of the author that this one shall encourage collectors to ask at least some of the questions.

Note to the illustrations:
All the pieces illustrated are from the museum at the
Wedgwood factory at Barlaston, with the exception of
Plates 4, 7, 9, 10, 16, 18, 22, 24, 29–31, 44–45, 47–49, 52, which
are from the City of Nottingham Museum and Art Gallery

2

Oval Plaque. Solid blue jasper with white bas-relief, 'The Judgement of Hercules' (also known as 'The Choice of Hercules'). Fine ormolu frame with ribbon tie loop. $9\frac{7}{8}'' \times 13''$.
Mark: WEDGWOOD & BENTLEY
Date: 1777

This superb plaque exists also in a larger rectangular form with additional reliefs flanking the central group of figures which represent Hercules choosing between Fame and Pleasure. In the example illustrated, the figure of Hercules is $7''$ high and the relief is $\frac{1}{2}''$ deep at the shoulder. The subject was modelled by William Hackwood and is listed in Wedgwood's Catalogue of 1787 as 'No. 69. Judgment of Hercules, modelled agreeably to Lord Salisbury's idea of representing the subject'. The term 'solid' is used to describe jasper of which the body is a uniform colour throughout. When jasper of one colour is dipped in a jasper clay solution of another colour it is known as 'jasper dip'. The remaining illustrations include many examples of both varieties.

17

3

Oval Medallion. Solid blue jasper with white bas-relief, 'Venus and Cupid'. Original brass frame. $6\frac{1}{2}'' \times 4\frac{3}{4}''$.
Mark: WEDGWOOD & BENTLEY
Date: 1778

Usually attributed to William Hackwood, this medallion is typical of those most popular for use in chimneypieces, though they were also marketed separately or in pairs for framing. Boulton and Fothergill made metal frames of the type illustrated at their Soho Works in Birmingham.

4

Oval Plaque. Pale grey-blue jasper, blue dip, and white bas-relief, 'Ganymede and the Eagle'. Height 7".
Mark: WEDGWOOD & BENTLEY
Date: 1778

No. 225 in the fifth edition of Wedgwood's *Catalogue*, this plaque or medallion is also mentioned in his letter to Bentley dated 14th April, 1778: 'We shall send you three pieces of jasper today from Sir Roger Newdigate's models,

which with the Eagle and Ganymede should be sent with our compliments.' The source of this medallion has been variously ascribed to a Roman sardonyx in the Marlborough collection and a relief illustrated in Bartoli and Bellori *Veterum Sepulcra* (Rome 1728), but it seems likely that Wedgwood took his model from the gem of this subject by James Tassie (see page 28).

5

Portrait Medallion. Edward Bourne, a bricklayer at Etruria. White jasper, blue dip. Black laurel and fluted jasper frame. To the right of the portrait head is a small bricklayer's trowel. The name 'EDᵂ BOURNE' impressed below the truncation. $6\frac{5}{8}'' \times 5\frac{5}{8}''$.
Marks: None   *Date:* 1779

One of the finest of Wedgwood's portrait medallions, modelled by William Hackwood in 1778. Wedgwood wrote to Bentley on 8th November, 1778, that he was sending him a portrait 'which you are to find out if your memory or Hackwood's skill are not deficient. It is a study, done for his amusement & improvement, & in my opinion a masterpiece.' Later in the month, evidently receiving Bentley's comments, he replied, 'Old Bourne's is the man himself, with every wrinkle, crink & cranny in the whole visage.'

This portrait has often been described as 'Edward Byrne', an error which arose from the name scratched on the back of a mould at the Wedgwood factory. Such mis-spellings are not rare among the factory records of the eighteenth century, others recorded including 'Coppol' (for Keppel) and 'Prusher' (for Prussia). The manuscript references, the impressed name, Hackwood's signature on the truncation of many of the surviving examples of this portrait, and the bricklayer's trowel, combine to make the identification of Bourne positive beyond any reasonable doubt.

6

Portrait Medallion. Queen Charlotte. Solid sage green jasper with white portrait relief and laurel border frame. Slotted at the back for hanging. $4\frac{1}{4}'' \times 3\frac{1}{4}''$.

Mark: WEDGWOOD
      MADE IN ENGLAND
      59 EC
Date: 1959

Originally modelled by William Hackwood in 1777 as a pair to his portrait of George III, this medallion has been reproduced several times in different colours during the past two hundred years. This modern example, though interesting and attractive, suffers from a lack of the crisp definition produced by undercutting, so noticeable a feature of the portrait of Edward Bourne (Plate 5). 'Undercutting' as the word suggests, is the method of hand-finishing after the portrait is removed from the mould, which sharpens the features and adds the chiselling on a plane horizontal (or parallel) to that of the medallion. This is a characteristic feature of all fine early portraits and of those small quantities finished by Bert Bentley in 1922.

7

Pair of Vases. Generally known as the Wine and Water vases. Solid blue and white jasper with finely modelled figures of a satyr and a triton. The wine vase is also decorated with a vine festoon and goat's head in high relief. The water vase has similar reliefs of an aquatic leaf festoon and marine monster's head. Each vase is fixed to the foot and plinth with a long metal screw. Height including plinth 15″. Plinth 4¼″ square.
Mark: Wine Vase. Wedgwood K

Mark: Water Vase. K (No Wedgwood mark)
Date: 1780

Originally supplied by Flaxman in 1775, probably as casts from antique models, these vases exist in comparatively large quantities in black basalt, having been reproduced frequently in the nineteenth century. In jasper they are exceptionally rare, and the few known examples belong to the first period.

8

Coffeepot. White jasper, blue dip, with bas-relief decoration from the series of designs 'Domestic Employment', by Lady Templetown. Height 8″.
Mark: WEDGWOOD A
Date: 1783

This piece bears many of the distinguishing marks of jasper of the best period: fine, even, engine-turned decoration to the lid and foot; crisp and well-chosen relief decoration; beauti-fully modelled acanthus terminals to the spout and handle; and, above all, an elegant and yet sturdy and practical form. The eccentric movement of the engine-turning lathe produced some of the most effective of all decorative designs on jasper.

9

Tea Canister and Cover. Solid blue jasper ornamented with reliefs of children at play. Height 3¾″. Diameter 3″.
Mark: WEDGWOOD 3
Date: 1783

'Canister' was the early name for the bottle-shaped containers which, filled with tea-leaves, were an essential part of the complete tea equipage of the eighteenth century. Hogarth's painting, 'The Walpole Family', shows this equipage —the cabriole-legged table, tea bowls and saucers, silver kettle and stand, and two tea canisters—in ritual use. Canisters, often of silver or porcelain, were later contained in caddies which, as tea became cheaper and required larger containers, finally replaced them. Porcelain or pottery canisters were made to match teasets, and Wedgwood produced them in Queensware, black basalt, and jasper.

24

10

Tea bowl and saucer. White jasper, lilac dip, with friezes of conventional foliage and rosette and scroll borders. Height 2″. Diameter $3\frac{1}{8}$″. Saucer diameter $5\frac{1}{4}$″.
Mark: Wedgwood 3
Date: 1785

Cream Jug. White jasper, lilac dip. Helmet shape with relief decoration of groups of women and children, insects, and 'The Young Seamstress' designed by Lady Templetown. Engine-turned foot. The terminal of the handle, where it is joined to the body of the jug, is the small shell much favoured by Wedgwood at this period. This helmet shape was very popular with silversmiths in the third quarter of the eighteenth century.

Mark: WEDGWOOD 3 0
Date: 1780

Lilac, rarest of all the early jasper colours, varies greatly in shade. It is often in a pale café-au-lait, and sometimes a clear pink. Colours of early jasper described as 'pink' and 'peach' are, in fact, variations of lilac caused generally by accidental changes of firing temperatures.

11

Custard Set. Four cups with covers on an octagonal tray. Solid blue jasper with white relief acanthus leaf decoration and shell terminals to the handles. Lapidary polished interiors to the cups. Tray 6″ × 6″.
Mark: WEDGWOOD 3
Date: 1784

Custard sets of this shape occur also in glass and silver of the period, and early-eighteenth-century soft-paste French porcelain. Wedgwood made similar sets in jasper, Queensware, and bone china until the end of the nineteenth century. The marks 0 and 3, impressed in the clay with the WEDGWOOD mark on early jasper, are thought to be associated with a particular craftsman as they appear only on pieces of excellent quality and approximately in the period 1780–1800. The 0 should not be confused with the elongated version of this letter impressed in jasper which also bears the marks of WEDGWOOD and ENGLAND. This elongated 0 is the personal mark of Bert Bentley and appears only on ware made between 1891 and 1936.

26

12

Early Morning Teaset. Teapot with cover, sugar bowl, cream jug, cup and saucer, and tray. Solid pale blue jasper with white reliefs from the 'Domestic Employment' designs by Lady Templetown and modelled by William Hackwood in 1783, and of boys at play. Tray $13\frac{3}{4}'' \times 11''$. Teapot height $4\frac{1}{2}''$.

Marks: WEDGWOOD except the cream jug which is marked Wedgwood. All pieces except the cream jug and tray bear the additional mark: 3

Date: 1784

Apart from the tray, all the pieces in this set show the incised fluted pattern of engine-turning, most noticeable on the lid and foot of the teapot. The cup is a tea bowl, without handle, and has a lapidary polished interior. The sugar bowl has a narrow line of white jasper inlaid in the foot, an extremely rare decorative feature.

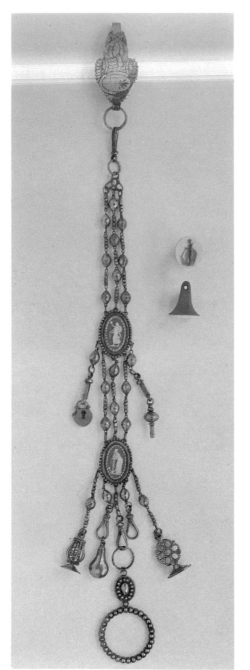

13

Cut steel chatelaine, or fob chain, mounted with two double-sided blue and white jasper cameos ornamented with bas-reliefs of 'Fortune' and 'Hope', and 'Fortune' and 'a Bacchante' respectively. Gentlemen's 'accoutrements' attached to the chain include an eye glass, miniature padlock and key, and several seals. The chain is linked to a steel waist clip with engraved patera and cornucopia design. Length 17″.
Mark: None visible
Date: 1785–90

Two shank seals of dark blue jasper with white dip and intaglio 'Diana'. Length 1″.
Marks: None visible.
Date: 1780

Intaglios (with incised or sunk design as opposed to decoration in relief) were much in demand towards the end of the eighteenth century both for use as seals and in collections reproducing famous antique gems. James Tassie, a Scottish modeller working in London, invented a form of glass paste which could be coloured, and cast or moulded to imitate gem stones with either intaglio or relief decoration. His fine cameo work competed seriously with Wedgwood's, but they remained rivals on friendly terms and Wedgwood purchased many of Tassie's casts from gems and models for portraits for reproduction in jasper or basalt.

14

Rectangular frame of twenty-six cameos. A collection of various subjects, including several examples of three-colour jasper, a fine cut steel mount, and cameos with bevelled and lapidary polished edges. The cameos all belong to the period 1775–1800.

Perhaps the most interesting subjects in this small collection are the six examples of horses modelled by Edward Burch R.A. after drawings by George Stubbs. Stubbs was commissioned by Wedgwood to model two important plaques, 'The Frightened Horse' and 'The Fall of Phaeton', for reproduction in jasper, and also to paint a large family group of Josiah and his family. He also painted a number of portraits and animal subjects on Wedgwood creamware plaques.

The portrait in the corner of the frame is of George III. This shows the use of jasper dip, the bevelled and polished edge, and the effect of 'bleeding' which colours and shades the thinnest parts of the relief.

15

Open Salt Cellar. One of a pair. Solid blue jasper with bas-relief, 'The Dancing Hours'. White jasper line inlaid at rim. Lapidary polished interior. Height $2\frac{1}{8}''$. Diameter $3''$.
Mark: WEDGWOOD 3 S
Date: 1785

Open Salt Cellar. One of a pair. Solid blue jasper with white floral swags. Engine-turned. Lapidary polished interior. Height $1\frac{7}{8}''$. Diameter $2\frac{7}{8}''$.
Mark: WEDGWOOD 0 3
Date: 1785

There is a well-known and apocryphal story that the Dancing Hours group, one of the loveliest of all Wedgwood's bas-reliefs, was originally modelled by Flaxman with the figures naked, the design being copied from an antique model. This was considered improper and the Flaxman dancing girls were draped by Hackwood. In fact Flaxman's early model, from which the salt cellar illustrated was taken, was of draped figures, though there was certainly a bacchanalian freedom in their movements and an evident intention to allow the draperies to flow rather than to conceal. This design from a chimney-piece then in the Palazzo Borghese was first produced in 1778. The original moulds have disappeared, and the graceful, but more chaste, dancers produced since 1802 are the work of William Hackwood.

16

Plaque. Solid blue and white jasper, 'Sacrifice to Ceres'. Rectangular 11¾″ × 6″.
Mark: WEDGWOOD
Date: 1785

Designed and modelled by John Flaxman, this plaque or 'tablet' is typical of those used for the decoration of chimneypieces and friezes for the walls of rooms in the Adam style. In spite of the disapproval of certain eminent architects, among them Sir William Chambers, and Wedgwood's difficulty in persuading them to use his tablets in their designs, it is clear that no serious obstacle existed to the sale of plaques and medallions for the cabinets of collectors and the enrichment of chimney-

pieces. By August, 1778, Wedgwood was confident that he had conquered the difficulties in firing such large flat pieces and wrote to Bentley: 'Do you wish to have any tablets sent? or would you rather sell what you have first? We have a very perfect one from Mr. Flaxman's model, & have several more in hand of different subjects. You shall have a most glorious assortment for the opening of the next season of Tablets, friezes, & blocks, to go together in the composition of a chimneypiece. We can make the friezes of any length and very true and even . . . & when we have completed our present suit of tablets & their accompaniments for chimneypieces we will make another attack on the architects and hope to conquer.'

17

Custard Cups. Pear or tear shape (also sometimes described as 'comma'). Lilac jasper and blue jasper with white latticework. Height 2″. Length 2½″.

Custard cup with cover. Yellow jasper with white latticework and finely pierced cover. Height 2½″.
Mark: WEDGWOOD
Date: 1786

All jasper bas-relief decoration is moulded separately in a 'pitcher' mould and applied by hand ('sprigged on') to the piece to be ornamented while in a clay state known as 'cheese hard'. Damped with water, the two surfaces adhere and are fused together in firing. It is generally true that clay composi-

tions of a different coefficient of expansion under heat will not fuse in this way, and this prevents the ornamenting of basalt with jasper and vice versa. Considerable dexterity is required to apply the jasper ornaments without blurring the details, and special care and skill would be necessary in the application of the delicate trellis or latticework on these custard cups.

32

18

Can cup and saucer and matching cream jug with cover. White jasper with reliefs of green ivy leaves and lilac berries, and applied oval dark blue and white jasper cameos in a beaded border and suspended by a lilac ribbon. Cup height $2\frac{5}{8}''$. Saucer diameter $4\frac{1}{8}''$.

Marks: WEDGWOOD H
       Saucer WEDGWOOD
       Jug WEDGWOOD Z
Date: 1790

These highly translucent pieces are excellent examples of the rare white jasper, not to be confused with the early 'waxen jasper', which is opaque, or the later 'smear glaze' white ware, which is open-textured and, if unglazed, porous.

19

Bowl on Foot. Solid blue jasper with white ornaments, 'Bacchanalian Boys', designed by Lady Diana Beauclerk in 1783, and vine festoons. Lapidary polished interior. Height 5″. Diameter 8⅞″.
Mark: WEDGWOOD
Date: 1785

Lady Diana Beauclerk, like Lady Templetown and Miss Crewe, was an amateur artist who supplied Bartolozzi with subjects for engravings and also designed bas-reliefs for Wedgwood's modellers. Born in 1734, she was the daughter of the second Duke of Marlborough. She married Lord Bolingbroke in 1757 and, after the dissolution of that marriage, the celebrated wit, Topham Beauclerk. Walpole described a set of her drawings as 'incomparable' and 'sublime' but, although she was highly talented, his effusive praise must be taken as indicative more of his delight in fashionable society than of his taste in art. Many of the bas-reliefs generally described as 'Bacchanalian Boys' and 'Boys at Play' are the work of Diana Beauclerk.

20

Vase. Pale blue-grey jasper with white snake handles and bas-reliefs of 'Venus in her Chariot' and laurel and acanthus borders. Screwed base and plinth. Rare Chinese fret relief ornament to plinth. Height to top of handles $16\frac{1}{2}''$.
Mark: WEDGWOOD
Date: 1785

A finely proportioned vase in the grey-blue jasper often found to have been used for the best pieces of the period. Wedgwood was evidently well satisfied with the vase for he used an illustration of it in his catalogue of 1787. The design 'Venus in her Chariot drawn by Swans', an interesting example of the survival of baroque among the neo-classical ornaments, is adapted from the work of Charles Le Brun. In recent years some writers have attributed this design to Madame Vigée-Le Brun. This error springs, presumably, from a misunderstanding of Miss Meteyard's attribution to 'Le Brun', which was correctly but as laconically repeated by Mankowitz. Only Grant specifically mentions Charles Le Brun, though a comparison of this design with the different styles of the two artists leaves little room for doubt.

21

Tube for Opera Glass. White jasper, dark blue dip, and white bas-relief ornaments, 'Sacrifice to Hymen'. Height 2¼".
Mark: None visible
Date 1787

Single Lens Telescopic Opera Glass (Monocular). White jasper, dark blue dip, and white bas-relief ornaments, 'Marriage of Cupid and Psyche'. Ormolu and ivory mounts. Height 3".

Mark: None visible.
Date: 1787

'Sacrifice to Hymen' was modelled in 1776 by William Hackwood as a companion subject to 'Marriage of Cupid and Psyche' (see Plate 22). These subjects are found in all sizes as a pair for medallions or plaques or for the decoration of such pieces as candelabra.

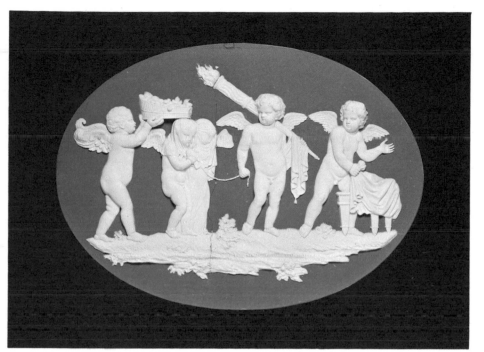

(*Illustrated: the version attributed to Flaxman*)

22

Plaque. White jasper, dark blue dip, white bas-relief ornament, 'The Marriage of Cupid and Psyche'. Oval 8″ × 11¾″.
Mark: WEDGWOOD *Date:* 1785

One of the most famous and most popular of all Wedgwood's relief subjects, 'The Marriage of Cupid and Psyche' was produced in all sizes from the largest plaque to the smallest cameo to be set in a ring. The subject was taken from a Graeco-Roman gem, a sardonyx, then in the Marlborough collection and now in the Museum of Fine Arts, Boston. Wedgwood produced three distinct versions of the subject, two of which show significant alterations from the original. Research by Dr. Lloyd Hawes (*The American Wedgwoodian* Vol. I No 2.) indicates that an engraving after Theodorus Netscher published in 1724 in *Pierres Antiques Gravées* served as the original for one altered version. The plaque most true to the original gem may have been taken from a sulphur cast by Tassie, who reproduced it in his glass paste, or from a study of the Marlborough gem. The third, attributed to Flaxman, gives more space to the figures and incorporates details from both other versions. The sixth edition of Wedgwood's catalogue contains 'grateful acknowledgements . . . to the duke of Marlborough for a cast from the exquisite gem in his grace's collection, the marriage of Cupid and Psyche'.

23

Teapot and Bowl, 'Brewster' shape. White jasper, pale green dip, and white bas-relief ornaments from the 'Domestic Employment' designs by Lady Templetown, modelled by William Hackwood in 1783. Engine-turned fluting to the bases. The teapot has a fluted handle and spout with acanthus and shell terminals. The bowl has a lapidary polished rim and interior. Diameter of bowl $7\frac{1}{4}''$.
Marks: Both marked WEDGWOOD 3
Date: 1786

Two pieces chosen to show the attractive combination of decoration obtained by using jasper dip and engine-turning with relief ornament. Wedgwood's engine-turning lathe was built for him by his friend Matthew Boulton in 1763. The eccentric movement of the machine enabled Wedgwood to design and produce diced, geometric, and fluted patterns on turned pieces both in solid colour and in jasper dip.

24

Covered chocolate cup and saucer. Solid blue jasper with white relief ornament of floral swags and inverted grasses. The blue ground is vertically engine-turned. Height $5\frac{3}{4}''$. Saucer diameter $6\frac{1}{2}''$.
Marks: Cup Wedgwood 5 S
        Saucer WEDGWOOD
Date: 1785

Chocolate as a beverage was introduced to Spain by Cortez but the secret was kept from the rest of Europe for a century. The first London 'Chocolate House' was opened in Bishopsgate in 1657, only five years after the first coffee house. In the days before effective journalism, political, military, and commercial news was most easily exchanged at these meeting places. 'The Windsor' at Charing Cross, advertised 'best chocolate at twelve pence the quart and the translation of the *Harlem Courant* soon after the post comes in'.

25

Four Scent Bottles

Glass bottle with gold screw top inset with black and white jasper cameo of a girl with doves, attributed to Lady Templetown (*top left*).

Oval bottle. White jasper, slate blue dip, and white relief ornament of a Greek warrior. Length 3½″ (*bottom left*).

Long octagonal bottle with gold screw top. Solid blue jasper, and white relief ornament of a Zephyr. 4″ × 1¾″ (*top right*).

Round bottle. White jasper, pale blue dip, and ornamented with relief portraits of George III and Queen Charlotte and laurel border (*bottom right*).

Marks: None visible
Dates: Circa 1785–90

40

26

Four Pin and Patch Boxes

Octagonal section wood pin-box with hinged lid set with blue and white jasper cameo under glass. Cut steel bead borders. The interior is fitted with a green velvet pincushion. Height $2\frac{3}{4}''$ (*top*).

Octagonal wood patch box with blue and white jasper cameo inset and borders of cut steel beads. Lined with cream velvet. Mirror set in lid. Length $4\frac{1}{2}''$.

Long oval ivory patch box with inset lilac, blue, and white jasper cameo, 'Sacrifice to Diana', and single border of cut steel beads. Lined with crimson velvet. The sliding base contains four silver and tortoiseshell card-shaped wafers, apparently the ace, two, three, and four of clubs. Length $3\frac{1}{2}''$.

Long oval ivory patch box with blue and white jasper cameo inset and cut steel bead border. Lined with pink velvet. Length $3\frac{1}{2}''$ (*bottom*).

Date: Circa 1790.

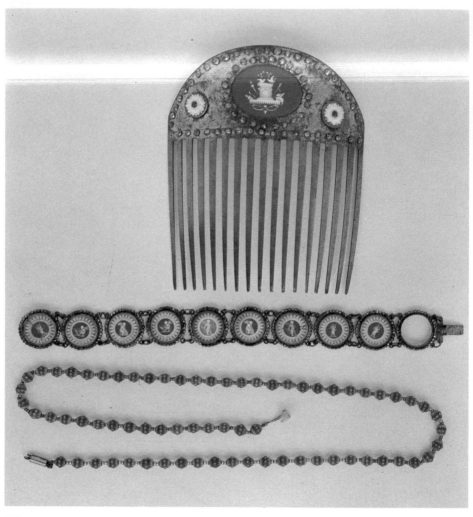

27

Steel comb set with two small rosettes and centre cameo of blue and white jasper. Length 4″.
Mark: WEDGWOOD   *Date:* 1786

Cut steel bracelet set with circular three-colour jasper cameos in lilac, blue, and white with cupid ornaments. Length 6″.

Mark: WEDGWOOD   *Date:* 1795

Small necklace of seventy-two matched dark blue and white jasper beads, each $\frac{1}{4}$″ long. Total length with metal link beads $19\frac{1}{2}$″.
Mark: None   *Date:* 1785

28

Cut steel chatelaine or fob chain set with two blue and white jasper cameos, 'A Conquering Hero' and 'Sacrifice to Peace' by John Flaxman. Length 8″.
Mark: WEDGWOOD
Date: 1786

Watch case of cut steel set with a blue and white jasper cameo of Apollo. The reverse side of the watch case is set with a miniature on ivory in the manner of Angelica Kauffmann.
Mark: WEDGWOOD
Date: 1786

The cut steel chatelaine is made up from cut steel beads of various sizes, threaded and attached to a hook by which it hung from the belt. Chatelaines were ornamental chains attached to the waist from which were hung such articles of domestic use as scissors, penknife, thimble-case, and button-hooks. Although they were in use towards the end of the eighteenth century, they became popular, particularly in steel, about 1830. In the 1870s they were more often made of oxidized silver or electroplate. (See also Plate 13.)

29

Candlestick. Solid blue and white jasper, modelled as the figure of a Triton grasping a whorled shell (which is usually surmounted by a white candle-holder). One of a pair. Height 11″.
Mark: WEDGWOOD
Date: 1785

The Triton figures, modelled for Wedgwood by John Flaxman but certainly from antique originals, are usually—and incorrectly—described as holding cornucopiae. Wedgwood was also an enthusiastic conchologist, and shell shapes appear in many of his bas-reliefs and also in patterns for Queensware.

30

Candlestick. Solid blue and white jasper. In the form of a tree trunk entwined with white vines and with the figure of a cupid with a basket of fruit, emblematic of autumn. Height 11″.
Mark: WEDGWOOD *Date:* 1785

One of a pair modelled by William Hackwood. The second figure, emblematic of winter, shows Cupid standing by a fire, the tree trunk being entwined with ivy leaves. Large free-standing pieces of this type were liable to distortion in firing and therefore costly to produce. They were never made in large quantities and are now particularly rare.

45

31

Can cup and saucer. White jasper, black dip, with vine festoon and laurel border, and applied lilac and white jasper cameo. Height $2\frac{7}{8}''$. Saucer diameter $4\frac{7}{8}''$.
Mark: Wedgwood
Date: 1790

Cream jug and cover. White jasper, black dip, ornamented with bas-relief group, 'Domestic Employment' (Woman Spinning with two children), designed by Lady Templetown. Base and cover engine-turned and with acanthus and lotus leaf borders.
Mark: WEDGWOOD H
Date: 1790

46

32

Teapot. Solid blue jasper with white handle, spout, finial, and bas-relief decoration. Height 8″.
Mark: WEDGWOOD 0
Date: 1790

A particularly fine and large teapot which combines a number of unusual features. The solid blue jasper ground is dimpled (or 'granulated'), providing an interesting textural contrast to the bas-reliefs designed by Lady Templetown. The split handle is decorated with an acanthus leaf, repeating the terminal of the overlapping leaf spout. The cover is surmounted by a splendidly modelled figure of Cupid with doves and a quiver of arrows, and the turned foot is decorated with strapwork. Sentimental 'domestic' scenes were popular as ornaments for jasper teasets. This is confirmed in a letter written by John Flaxman in 1782: 'According to the desire you expressed in the last letter you favoured me with I have designed some Groups of Children proper for bas-reliefs to decorate the sides of teapots.'

33

Wall Sconce. Pale blue jasper plaque, with white bas-relief of a Herculaneum figure, a female dancer playing cymbals, mounted in a beaded metal frame to form the backplate of a wall sconce. Matching pale blue and white jasper candle holders and drip trays are set in shaped metal arms. 15″ × 8″.
Mark : None visible
Date : 1785

One of the figures listed in the catalogue of 1788 as having been taken from models in the Lansdowne collection after paintings in the ruins of Herculaneum. Wedgwood made them in basalt, terra-cotta, and jasper prior to 1783 when they are first mentioned in his catalogue.

34

Round Dish. Solid blue jasper with white bas-relief group 'The Infant Academy' designed by Sir Joshua Reynolds in the centre, and leaf border. The dish is engine-turned to produce a shallow fluted effect between the centre ornament and the border. Diameter $9\frac{3}{4}''$.
Mark: WEDGWOOD 0 3
Date: 1790

Powder Box. Solid blue jasper with white bas-relief groups 'Poor Maria', 'Cupid's Parade', and 'Cupids at Play', all designed by Lady Templetown. Engine-turned foot and lid.
Mark: WEDGWOOD 3
Date: 1785

Sir Joshua Reynolds painted portraits

of Josiah Wedgwood and his wife, Sarah, which are now at the Wedgwood factory at Barlaston. Wedgwood's jasper portrait medallion of Reynolds was modelled by Flaxman, and a version of it, on a green ground, is fixed to Sir Joshua's easel at Burlington House. The design appearing on this dish, 'The Infant Academy', was modelled by William Hackwood in 1785 for a tea service presented to Reynolds by Wedgwood.

Bell Pulls.

Oviform, white jasper, pale green dip, and white acanthus and lotus leaf ornaments. Height $2\frac{3}{4}''$ (*above*).

Oviform, white jasper, blue dip, dipped a second time in white, engine-turned and incised to produce a blue intaglio pattern (*below*).
Marks: None visible
Date: 1785

An almost identical shape, hollowed inside, was also used for scent or smelling bottles, fitted with silver or gold screw stoppers. These bell pulls were intended to be attached to the long sashes or bell-cords which hung on the walls and were connected by a long and complicated series of wires to bells in the servants' quarters. The blue bell pull is an interesting example of the use of a second jasper dip, a rare form of decoration and one which is not always immediately obvious.

Cameo. Pale blue jasper with darker blue dip and white bas-relief, 'Bourbonnais Shepherd', mounted as a buckle in cut steel by Boulton and Fothergill. Overall size $2\frac{3}{4}'' \times 2''$.
Mark: WEDGWOOD
Date: 1785

Cameo. White jasper, blue dip, and white bas-relief, 'Poor Maria', mounted as a buckle. The mount, by Boulton and Fothergill, is of cut steel with beads of steel, glass, and blue and white jasper. Overall height $3\frac{1}{2}''$.
Mark: WEDGWOOD
Date: 1785

Both bas-relief subjects were designed by Lady Templetown and modelled by William Hackwood. Elizabeth, Lady Templetown, was born in 1747, the daughter of Shuckburgh Boughton of Poston. In 1769 she married Clothworthy Upton, who was created Baron Templetown in 1776. Her designs for Wedgwood were created between 1783 and 1787 and appear to have included most of the 'domestic' subjects, though it is not always possible to differentiate between her work and that of Miss Crewe. 'Poor Maria', inspired by Sterne's character, was adapted from a painting by Joseph Wright of Derby, who also completed several commissioned paintings for Josiah Wedgwood.

37

Teapot. 'Empire' shape. Solid grey-blue jasper with white bas-relief groups, 'Charlotte at the Tomb of Werther' and 'Sportive Love', designed by Lady Templetown and modelled by William Hackwood in 1785. Engine-turned foot and lid. The fluted spout and handle terminate in acanthus leaf mouldings. Height 6″.
Mark: Wedgwood
Date: 1790

Goethe's *Die Leiden des Jungen Werthers,* which inspired the bas-relief illustrated, was published in 1774 and it is interesting to find its influence recognized in English pottery after only fifteen years.

38

Vase with cover. Solid blue jasper with white relief ornaments. White jasper tripod supports in the form of rams' heads and feet, festoons of flowers, laurel borders, and lotus flower knob to domed cover. One of a pair. Height including knob 9".
Mark: WEDGWOOD
Date: 1789

Wedgwood was justly proud of his vases, and wrote of them to his patron,

Sir William Hamilton, 'One thing I persuade myself you will observe, that they have been objects of very great labour and time, every ornament and leaf being made in a separate mould, then laid upon the vase with great care & accuracy, and afterwards wrought over again upon the vase itself by an artist equal to the work.'

39

Two vases with covers. White jasper with black dip and white bas-reliefs of 'Venus in her Chariot' and 'Sacrifice to Ceres'. White Etruscan scroll handles, screwed feet and plinths. Heights 12″ and 10½″.

Marks: WEDGWOOD H and
WEDGWOOD   *Date:* 1790

These two vases are from a set of three designed as a *garniture de cheminée*. They were also used with pedestals of the design illustrated in Plate 50. The mark 'H' appearing on the plinth of the larger vase has been attributed to William Hackwood, but there is no evidence to support this.

54

40

Candelabra. Cut glass and black and white jasper drums mounted in ormolu. The drops are of yellow and white glass. Height 11″.
Mark: WEDGWOOD
Date: 1790

Matthew Boulton (1728–1809) was an engineer. He and James Watt were in partnership as steelworkers and makers of steam engines, but he was also in partnership with James Fothergill at the Soho Works, Birmingham, as a merchant and dealer in ornamental metalwork. He made cut steel, pinchbeck, pressed brass, and ormolu mounts and frames for Wedgwood. After a visit to the Soho Works in 1776, Wedgwood wrote to Bentley, 'I had no conception of the quantity of D'Or Moulu they have sold, chiefly abroad.'

Buttons. Pair of white jasper, blue dip, cameos of Hercules subjects, set in silver as buttons. Diameter $1\frac{3}{4}''$.
Mark: None visible
Date: 1790

Clock Pendulum. Dark blue and white jasper circular cameo set in cut steel beaded mount as a pendulum. The cameo is ornamented with the signs of the zodiac, originally supplied to Wedgwood by Mrs. Mary Landre in 1774 and modelled by Hackwood. They were used as a frieze on certain fine black basalt vases of the Wedgwood and Bentley period before being reduced in size for use in cameo borders and for the decoration of jasper pieces. Recently they have been reproduced as separate figures in bas-relief for setting in cufflinks and brooches. The use of jasper bas-relief was particularly suitable for the signs of the zodiac as the word derives from the Greek *zodion*, meaning the sculptured figure of an animal. Wedgwood cameos were much used for the decoration of clocks, both in England and in France, and there are examples of the work of the great clockmaker, Benjamin Vulliamy, which incorporate jasper cameos or medallions in the case design; but the use of cameos to ornament the working parts of clocks was rare.
Mark: None visible
Date: 1800

42

Chessmen. Solid blue and white jasper. King, queen, bishop, knight, castle, and three pawns. Height of queen $3\frac{1}{2}''$.
Mark: WEDGWOOD
Date: 1790

This set of chessmen was designed and modelled by John Flaxman in 1785, and his original drawing is in the Wedgwood Museum at Barlaston. Many complete sets were sold; no fewer than one hundred and thirty between 1785 and 1795, and the pieces were also reproduced during the nineteenth century. It is surprising, therefore, to find that they are now so rare. Some attractive variations of colour were used, and dark blue, lilac, and green dip bases are found with solid white figures. The figure of the queen is said to portray Mrs. Siddons in the character of Lady Macbeth, and it certainly bears a strong resemblance to the Wedgwood portrait medallion of her, also modelled by Flaxman in 1784. Complete sets are seldom offered for sale, but it is still occasionally possible to find single pieces.

43

Pair of Incense Burners. White jasper, deep blue dip, solid white dolphin tripod supports, finely perforated lids, foliage swags, and applied rosettes. Height $5\frac{1}{4}''$.
Mark: WEDGWOOD
Date: 1800

This model also exists in Wedgwood black basalt of the first period. Incense, or pastille, burners made of porcelain or earthenware were popular during the eighteenth and nineteenth centuries for burning *cassolette* perfumes—powdered willow-wood charcoal mixed with fragrant oils and gum arabic—which helped to disguise the odours of insufficiently aired rooms and their seldom-washed occupants. Wedgwood's elegant tripods and their finely perforated covers are the aristocratic counterparts of the gaily enamelled cottages and churches made by the Staffordshire potteries in the nineteenth century.

44

Vase and cover. White jasper, greenish-buff dip, solid blue clouds, and white relief representing 'The Apotheosis of Homer'. Solid white jasper plinth with Chinese fret decoration. Height 18″.
Mark: WEDGWOOD
Date: 1790

Designed by John Flaxman in 1784 with relief subjects modelled by him six years earlier, this vase is, with the single exception of the copies of the Portland Vase (Plate 1), the finest of all the Wedgwood vases. Wedgwood presented a version in blue and white jasper to the British Museum, and wrote to Sir William Hamilton that it was 'the finest and most perfect I have ever made'. This example is unique in colour and may have been a trial piece.

45

Can cup and saucer. White jasper, sage green dip, four decorative bands of applied blue squares and green quatrefoils, and three bas-relief groups of 'Venus Bound', 'A Warrior', and 'Nymphs' in compartments divided by foliage. The saucer is ornamented with one band of applied blue squares and green quatrefoils and a border of rosettes separated by foliage. Height $2\frac{5}{8}''$. Saucer diameter $4\frac{3}{4}''$.
Mark: Cup WEDGWOOD H
        Saucer Wedgwood
Date: 1790

Can cup and saucer. White jasper, blue dip, and four bas-relief groups in separated compartments. Leaf borders. Height $2\frac{7}{8}''$. Saucer diameter $4\frac{7}{8}''$.

Mark: WEDGWOOD A
Date: 1820

The squared border of the first example, achieved by the application of separately moulded pieces in blue and green to a white background, should not be confused with the diced pattern (Plate 55) which is produced by a different technique using the engine-turning lathe.

Tea bowl and saucer. White jasper, pale green dip, and small bas-reliefs of boys at play. Lapidary polished rim and interior to bowl. Very translucent. Height 2½″.
Mark: Bowl WEDGWOOD 0
Saucer WEDGWOOD 3
Date: 1785

Teacup and saucer. White jasper, lilac dip, and bas-reliefs of children by Lady Diana Beauclerk. Lapidary polished interior to cup. Shell terminal to handle. Very translucent. Height 2½″.
Mark: Cup WEDGWOOD 3 0
Saucer WEDGWOOD 3 H
Date: 1785

Can cup and saucer. White jasper, lilac dip, with applied lilac squares and green quatrefoils. Height 2½″.
Mark. WEDGWOOD 3
Date: 1790

47

Court Sword. Steel hilt and guard of cut, shaped, and polished beads, the hilt decorated with four blue and white jasper cameos, and the guard with eight blue and white jasper beads. Blade length $32\frac{1}{2}''$. Full length of sword in vellum scabbard $38\frac{1}{2}''$.

An extremely fine and rare example of eighteenth-century craftsmanship, probably made in Wolverhampton about 1790, and reputed, on doubtful authority, to have belonged to Beau Brummel.

48

Tea Caddy. Ribbed ivory applied to tortoise-shell, each facet of the octagon being ornamented with a blue and white jasper cameo. Gold mounts. Height 5¾".
Date: 1800

The word 'caddy' is thought to be a corruption of the Malayan *'kati'*, a measured quantity of about 1⅓ pounds, and first appears as 'tea cadet' and 'tea cade'. Sheraton's catalogue of 1803 mentions that 'the word caddy is now applied to various kinds of tea chests of square, octagon and circular shape'. Pitt estimated that less than half of the thirteen million pounds of tea consumed in Britain in 1784 had paid the heavy duty to which it was liable. Even the estimable Parson Woodforde, author of *The Diary of a Country Parson*, was glad to buy his tea from 'Andrews the smuggler'.

49

Two-handled cup. Solid blue jasper with white handles and bas-relief ornaments, 'The Young Seamstress' and 'The Reading Lesson', designed by Lady Templetown. Engine-turned lower half of the bowl, and turned foot. Height 4″.
Mark: WEDGWOOD S
Date: 1790

A 'cabinet piece', not intended for use, and closely following the design of silver goblets of a slightly earlier period, metal fluting being replaced by engine-turning.

50

Square pedestal. White jasper, black dip, with bas-reliefs of 'Venus and Cupid', 'Cupid and Psyche', and 'Hope', designed and modelled by William Hackwood. Height 7″.
Mark: WEDGWOOD
Date: 1796

Square bulb pot. Solid blue jasper with white ornaments and bas-relief of 'Nemesis', 'Aesculapius', and 'Diomedes', designed and modelled by William Hackwood. Height 7″.
Mark: WEDGWOOD
Date: 1796

A few of Wedgwood's early jasper pieces were designed for more than one purpose. The square pedestal illus-

trated could be used in conjunction with suitable vases (those shown in Plate 39 were often sold with this pedestal); or, with a flat perforated flower holder, as a vase; or, as illustrated, with a shaped holder, as a bulb pot.

65

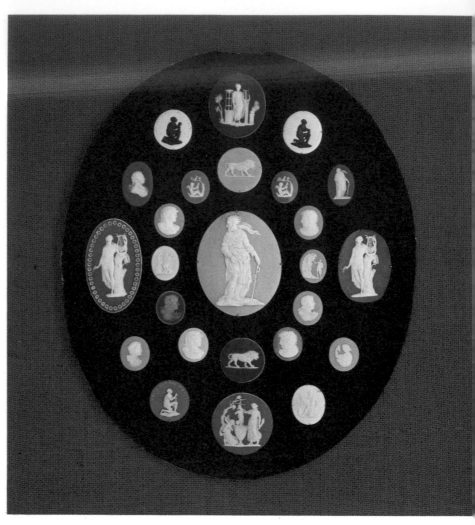

51

Oval frame of twenty-five jasper cameos, illustrating the many different coloured grounds, including yellow, brown, green, black, blue, and lilac, and also an interesting 'trial' piece of green on black. Many of these pieces are marked as trials and were never produced for regular sale.

Among the cameos are three versions of the famous 'Slave medallion', modelled by Hackwood in 1787 and adopted as a seal by the committee of the Society for the Abolition of Slavery. An inscription round the edge reads, 'AM I NOT A MAN AND A BROTHER?'.

52

Chamber candlestick. Fluted white jasper, pale green dip, and white leaf ornament. Loop for extinguisher. Height 3½″ (*left*).
Mark: WEDGWOOD
Date: 1810

Chamber candlestick. Fluted white jasper, blue dip, and white leaf ornament. Height 2¼″ (*centre*)
Mark: WEDGWOOD
Date: 1810

Candlestick. Solid blue jasper with white acanthus and anthemion ornament. Engine turned. Height 5½″ (*right*).
Mark: WEDGWOOD
Date: 1790

Chamber candlesticks, so named because they were intended to light the owner to bed, were usually designed with small loop carrying handles and often with cone-shaped extinguishers. These are sometimes described as 'snuffers', but this is a word more properly applied to the metal scissors-like implements used both for extinguishing candles and for trimming their wicks.

53

Trophy Plate. White jasper, green dip, heavily ornamented with white reliefs and lilac quatrefoils, with centre cameo of Aurora. Diameter 8¾".
Mark: WEDGWOOD
Date: 1860

The cameo of Aurora was originally modelled by Hackwood in 1773. Approximately one hundred and seventy separate reliefs are used to ornament the trophy plate, the precise number depending upon the centre and border decorations chosen. As a design it is open to criticism, but there can be no doubt of the technical expertise required for its production. It has, nevertheless, been reproduced successfully by Wedgwood within the past ten years.

54

Teapot and cream jug. White jasper, turquoise dip, and white bas-reliefs of a 'Sacrifice' subject. 146 Shape.
Mark: WEDGWOOD
Date: 1880

Turquoise jasper was introduced as a dip in 1875 but continued in production only for a few years. The quality of this ware does not compare favourably with early jasper, the body being granular and the applied figures less crisply defined, but the colour is rare. The pieces illustrated show a number of transitional features: the solid white jasper spout with leafage terminal was soon to be replaced by plainer spouts of the same colour as the main body of the teapot; but the glazing of the interior of the teapot indicates that it was intended for use. Although non-porous, the interiors of jasper pieces intended for use with liquids have usually been glazed during the past century. This is an indication of period which, while inconclusive by itself, may be useful to confirm other indicators.

55

Tobacco Box. White jasper, black dip, diced and decorated with applied yellow quatrefoils and running laurel borders. Height 8".
Mark: WEDGWOOD
Date: 1880

An example of the diced pattern pro-duced by the use of the engine-turning lathe, the chequered effect being the result of cutting through the dip to the ground colour and not achieved by the application of coloured squares as in Plates 45 and 46.

56

Teapot. White jasper, crimson dip, and white bas-relief ornament of a 'Sacrifice' subject. Glazed interior. Height 3½″.
Mark: WEDGWOOD ENGLAND
Date: 1928

Spill Vase. White jasper, crimson dip, and white acanthus and tall lily bas-relief ornament, patrician border, rams' heads, and rose swags. Height 7½″.
Mark: WEDGWOOD
        MADE IN ENGLAND
        and elongated 0
Date: 1930

The spill vase is the work of A. H. (Bert) Bentley, who worked as a modeller at the Etruria factory from 1891 to 1936.

The quality of his modelling and under-cutting is easily recognizable in comparing the two pieces illustrated. Crimson jasper dip was produced for a short period between 1925 and 1932, though experimental pieces appeared some ten years earlier. It was never available in large quantities owing to the tendency of the colour to 'bleed' in firing and stain the white relief ornaments. It is consequently rare.

57

Chessmen. Solid blue and white jasper. King, queen, bishop, knight, castle, and three pawns. Height of King $5\frac{1}{2}''$.
Mark: WEDGWOOD
      MADE IN ENGLAND
Date: 1969

Part of a set of chessmen designed by Arnold Machin R.A. in 1938 and produced before 1940 in different bodies including basalt, jasper, Queensware, and bone china. A Wedgwood portrait medallion of Queen Elizabeth II is based on Machin's design for British postage stamps, and a number of his figures and groups have been produced in Queensware and basalt. More than any sculptor or modeller associated with the British pottery industry during the past forty years, Arnold Machin exemplifies, in his work, the earthy humour and simplicity of traditional Staffordshire modelling. The simplicity is deceptive: his consummate craftsmanship, displayed more obviously in his serious 'Academy' work, and his thorough understanding of his medium, are directly in the tradition of the sculptor-modellers employed or commissioned by Wedgwood in the eighteenth century, but his fresh wit and originality are of our own time.

58

Mug. Solid black jasper with white relief lettering, 'A SOUVENIR', each letter containing a cameo. Wide glazed band and glazed interior. Capacity 1 pint.

Designed in 1966 by Professor Richard Guyatt, head of the School of Graphic Design at the Royal College of Art, this 'Sporting Mug' received a special commendation and design award from the Council of Industrial Design. In each letter of the relief is set a cameo view of a famous British sporting centre: St. Andrews, Cowes, Brands Hatch, Twickenham, Wimbledon, Lord's, Epsom, Wembley, and Henley. This souvenir mug was originally introduced in a limited edition of 500, each piece being numbered in a special backstamp describing the cameos.

TRADE MARKS

wedgwood	Probably the first mark. Supposed to have been used by Josiah Wedgwood at Burslem 1759–1769.

WEDCWOOD	This is a very rare mark, used at the Bell Works 1764–1769

WEDGWOOD Wedgwood	Used in varying sizes from 1759–1769.

 The circular stamp, without the inner and outer rings, and without the word Etruria is doubtless the earliest form of the Wedgwood and Bentley stamp, 1769.

 This mark, with the word Etruria, was fixed in the corner, inside the plinth of old basalt vases. It is sometimes found on the pedestal of a bust or large figure. 1769–1780.

 This circular stamp, with an inner and outer line, was always placed around the screw of the basalt, granite and Etruscan vases, but is never found on Jasper vases. 1769–1780.

Wedgwood & Bentley (script)	Unique script mark, Wedgwood & Bentley, 1769–1780.
Wedgwood & Bentley 356	Mark used on Wedgwood & Bentley intaglios, with the catalogue number varying in size, 1769–1780.
W. & B.	Very small intaglios were sometimes marked W&B with the catalogue number, or simply with the number only, 1769–1780.
Wedgwood & Bentley (circular)	Rare mark found only on chocolate and white seal intaglios, usually portraits made of two layers of clay with the edges polished for mounting, 1769–1780.
WEDGWOOD & BENTLEY Wedgwood & Bentley	These marks, varying in size, are found upon busts, granite and basalt vases, figures, plaques, medallions and cameos, from the largest tablet to the smallest cameo. 1769–1780.
WEDGWOOD Wedgwood WEDGWOOD WEDGWOOD	Varying in size, these marks are attributed to the period after Bentley's death (1780) and probably used for a time after Josiah's death (1795)

75

Trade Marks *continued*

WEDGWOOD & SONS	Very rare mark used for a short period in 1790.

JOSIAH WEDGWOOD Feb. 2nd 1805	Mark of Josiah Wedgwood II. Supposedly a new partnership or change in the firm. Found only on some basalt tripod incense burners. It may be the date when the design was first registered, 1805. Sometimes '2nd Feby' appears instead of 'Feb. 2'.

WEDGWOOD	The mark upon the bone china or porcelain, made 1812–1822, always printed either in red, blue, or in gold.

WEDGWOOD WEDGWOOD	From 1769 to the present day this mark has been impressed in the clay on Queensware, or printed in colour. In recent times the words Etruria and Barlaston and the name of the pattern have in many cases been printed in addition to the trade mark. From 1780, ornamental Jasper, Black Basalt, cane, terra cotta, and Queensware are always marked with this stamp. The name 'England' was added in 1891.

WEDGWOOD
ETRURIA
WEDGWOOD
ETRURIA
Wedgwood
Etruria

These marks are rarely found on pieces of a very high character. Adopted about 1840 but used for only a short period.

WEDGWOOD

This mark, now in use on bone china, was adopted in 1878 when the manufacture of bone china was revived. It is printed in various colours.

ENGLAND

England was added to the mark Wedgwood in 1891 to comply with the American Customs Regulation known as the McKinley Tariff Act.

WEDGWOOD
Bone China
MADE IN ENGLAND

Mark used today on bone china, developed from mark of 1878.

WEDGWOOD

This mark, printed in colour, is being used today on Queensware, starting in 1940.

GLOSSARY

BAS-RELIEF. Embossed, carved, or cast decoration or ornament in low relief. Also applied to jasper 'dip' as a general description.

BISCUIT OR BISQUE. Pottery or porcelain which has been fired but not glazed.

BODY. Name given to the composite materials of which potter's clay is made, but normally only used when referring to earthenware or stoneware. The term paste is used for porcelain or china.

CAMEO. Ornament in relief as distinguished from intaglio, and specifically that which is in one colour on a ground of a different colour.

CASTING. Process of forming shapes by pouring slip (see page 79) into dry plaster moulds which immediately absorb moisture from the slip. When sufficient thickness of the clay has adhered to the inside of the mould the remaining slip is poured out and the mould set to dry, after which the form is removed from the mould.

ENGINE-TURNING LATHE. A lathe equipped with an eccentric motion, such as was built for Josiah Wedgwood by Matthew Boulton in 1763. By means of this lathe, geometric, diced, and fluted decorations were incised on vases and other pieces.

FIRING. Process of transforming clay into pottery by burning it in a special oven or kiln.

GLAZE. Glassy preparation applied to the surface of biscuit ware to render it impervious to liquids.

SALT GLAZE. Transparent hard glaze with pitted or 'orange peel' surface, produced by throwing rock salt into the kiln from above at the maximum degree of heat.

SMEAR GLAZE. Semi-glaze or thin deposit on the surface of pottery, produced by smearing the inside of the saggar (see page 79) with the glaze.

INTAGLIO. Sunken or incised design, the reverse of cameo.

JASPER, JASPER DIP. Dense white vitrified stoneware body of nearly the same properties as porcelain. Translucent when thinly potted. When coloured throughout the body it is called solid jasper. When the body is dipped in a solution of another coloured jasper it is called jasper dip (or bas-relief ware).

MOULD. Cast, usually plaster composition, taken from an original model so that many reproductions may be made. The block mould is taken from the original model; a case mould in relief is taken from the block mould; and from the case mould the potter's working mould (intaglio) is made. From this the required cast piece is produced. Working moulds are reproduced from the case mould as needed.

ORNAMENTING. Process of applying relief decoration to ware while still in the plastic state. Clay is pressed into 'pitcher' moulds already cast in intaglio with the decoration required. The clay relief is lifted out and applied to the ware after moistening the surface. The ornament is fixed by gentle pressure of the craftsmen's fingers. A sensitive touch is necessary to preserve the fine detail of the applied ornament.

SAGGAR. The fire-clay container in which the wares are placed within the oven to protect them from direct contact with the flames.

SLIP. Clay watered down to a creamy consistency.

STONEWARE. Opaque, vitrified, hard body fired at high temperature. Impervious to water without glazing. The connecting link between earthenware and porcelain. Jasper is a unique variant.

THROWING. Process of making ware on a potter's wheel. The name comes from the action of throwing a ball of soft clay down upon the revolving wheel. The ball is then centred on the wheel and worked up with the hands.

TURNING. Process of shaping on a horizontal lathe similar to that used in the turning of wood.

FURTHER READING

A comprehensive bibliography could fill a small volume by itself. This short list includes the important standard works on Wedgwood and a number of others which contain valuable information not available elsewhere.

BARNARD, Harry. *Chats on Wedgwood Ware* London 1924; Stokes & Co., New York

BURTON, William. *Josiah Wedgwood and his Pottery* Cassell, London 1922

BUTEN, Harry M. *Wedgwood Counterpoint*; *Wedgwood and Artists* 1960; *Wedgwood ABC* 1964; *Wedgwood Rarities* 1969; Buten Museum of Wedgwood publications, Merion, Pennsylvania

FARRER, Katherine E. (Ed.) *Wedgwood's Letters to Bentley* London 1903

FINER, Ann, and SAVAGE, George (Ed.) *The Selected Letters of Josiah Wedgwood* Cory, Adams & Mackay, London 1965

GRANT, M. H. *The Makers of Black Basaltes* London 1910. Reprinted, Holland Press, London 1967

HONEY, W. B. *Wedgwood Ware* Faber & Faber, London 1948; Van Nostrand, New York

KELLY, Alison. *The Story of Wedgwood* Compiled in association with Josiah Wedgwood & Sons Ltd., Faber & Faber, London 1962; Viking Press, New York 1962

MACHT, Carol. *Classical Wedgwood Designs* M. Barrows & Co., New York 1957

MANKOWITZ, Wolf. *Wedgwood* Batsford 1953; E. P. Dutton, New York 1953; Spring Books, London–New York 1966

—— *The Portland Vase and the Wedgwood Copies* Andre Deutsch, London 1952

METEYARD, Eliza. *Life of Josiah Wedgwood* London 1865. Reprinted, Kelley, New York 1969; David and Charles, Newton Abbott 1970

RATHBONE, Frederick. *Old Wedgwood* London 1898

SMILES, Samuel. *Josiah Wedgwood* John Murray, London 1894